Amusing Grace

The Funny Side of Faith

Publications International, Ltd.

Jonny Hawkins has been cartooning professionally since 1986. His work has been in over 600 publications and in hundreds of books. He creates several cartoon-a-day calendars including *Medical Cartoon-a-Day, Fishing, Teachers,* and more. He lives in Sherwood, Michigan, with his wife, Carissa, and their three young children. He is available at jonnyhawkins2nz@yahoo.com.

Louis Weber, CEO
Publications International, Ltd.
7373 North Cicero Avenue
Lincolnwood, Illinois 60712

ISBN-13: 978-1-4508-4928-9
ISBN-10: 1-4508-4928-8

Manufactured in USA.

8 7 6 5 4 3 2 1

Everybody needs a good laugh, and if you know what you're looking for, you can find humor almost anywhere. Funny things are happening all around us, even in church!

Great thinkers over the centuries have wondered whether God has a sense of humor. The answer seems obvious: He created human beings with a sense of humor, so he must have had his own sense of humor to begin with. And if that's not enough proof for you, just think about the dodo bird for a few minutes.

These cartoons will draw a good number of chuckles from you, and maybe even a belly laugh or two. The biggest giggles may well come if you recognize yourself in any of them. So sit back, enjoy the fun, and see if anything looks familiar.

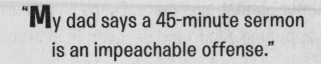

"My dad says a 45-minute sermon is an impeachable offense."

"**Y**ou gotta stop taking leaps of faith."

"**C**ount the cost before you sit down.
We metered the back pew."

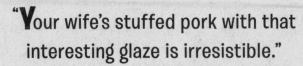

"The new sound system? Awesome."

"**A**nd now, an update from our missionary in Australia..."

"**Y**ou won the Humilitarian of the Year award! How come you didn't tell anyone?!"

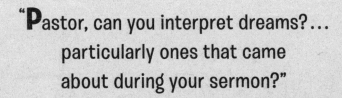

"**P**astor, can you interpret dreams?...
particularly ones that came
about during your sermon?"

Sourcreek Community's annual quirky hat day takes on a life of its own.

"**A**nd to ensure your confidence as our new pastor, we'll have the beloved former pastor reassigned to the back pew."

"**P**astor can't come to the phone right now. He's...uh...online."

"**W**hat did you expect in Hog Heaven?"

"I'm happy to join the Hospital Visitation Group ... I'm just a little concerned about catching something."

"**P**oint me in the direction of your gossips and back biters…"

"I would like to lay up treasures in heaven. Do you know the present conversion rate?"

a motion that even if nobody
this motion, it passes anyway."

"I like our new pastor, but sometimes
he does seem a little judgmental."

"I was going to preach on self-confidence, but I've had second thoughts..."

"I like our new pastor, but sometimes he does seem a little judgmental."

"**S**quirming or non-squirming?"

"I make a motion that even if nobody seconds this motion, it passes anyway."

"I was going to preach on self-confidence, but I've had second thoughts..."

"**M**y husband goes forward every Sunday because he has an altar ego."

"These are the final figures for the building fund expenses."

"**F**lattop Merkins" takes his job as head usher to the next level.

"**O**h, it's nothing... I'm trying to get rid of some leftovers... it's Beanie Baby casserole."

"**S**ince we don't have a sloped floor, we stack chairs in the last few rows for visual purposes."

"**Y**ou were my lone parishioner taking sermon notes. Turns out you were just doing crossword puzzles?"

"We had a minor disagreement."

"**Y**our sermon today touched my heart, Pastor. The only thing is...I'm ticklish."

"...**A**nd Mabel, here, runs the mixing board."

"**E**very sermon is a cliffhanger!"

"**H**ow much scripture memory does it have?"

The new family showed signs
of being unapproachable.

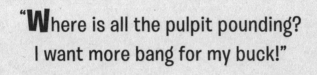

"**W**here is all the pulpit pounding?
I want more bang for my buck!"

It was apparent Reverend Haddleburg had gotten a faith lift.

WOW. A BARN-SHAPED CHURCH! DOES THAT AT ALL AFFECT THE PEOPLE'S MENTALITY?
NO. MY SHEEP DON'T FIND IT TOO BA-A-A-A-D. AND IF THEY DO, WE ASK THEM TO MOO-OO-OO-VE.
JONNY HAWKINS

"I'm a praying mantis, yes—but, right now I'm meditating."

"Huh, a chain epistle."

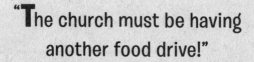

"I was cleansed from sin, and today I go through the rinse cycle...I get baptized."

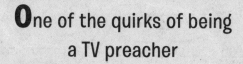

One of the quirks of being a TV preacher

"**Y**our wife called. She wants you to pick the little heathen up from the Thompsons on your way home."

"**U**nlike our Lord, the dough didn't rise."

When Pastor Woodley made a good point, his ushers employed what would become a trademark: the chest-bump.

"Before I call up God,
what time is it in Heaven?"

For ready-made street preaching, and to prepare his sermons on-the-go, Pastor Goebert ordered himself a Segway Pulpit Mover.

"**N**ow that was a four-alarm sermon!"

"**W**e've found a way to cut costs for our new building project."

"I'm taking you off potlucks and putting you on prayer and fasting."

"**C**an I download your special
music onto my iPod?"

Pastor Wilbur is thinking of taking
the word "vacation" out of
Vacation Bible School.

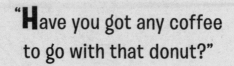

"No. No exit polls here."

The weekly challenges of a mega-church pastor

Sam Collins stirs up the waters by doing a cannonball at his baptism.

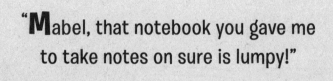

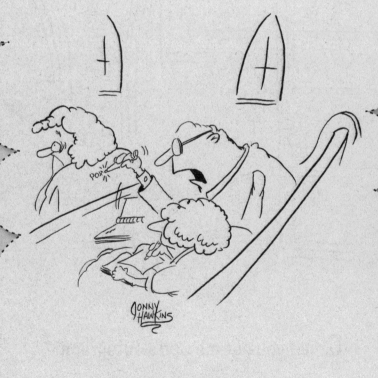

"**C**ould you get me God's autograph?"

Musician Aaron Mullins realizes that he mistakenly thought they requested "spacial music."

"I heard you have great subwoofers."

108

"The Reverend used to be a geometry teacher. That's why he goes off on so many tangents."

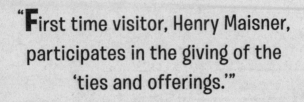

"**F**irst time visitor, Henry Maisner,
participates in the giving of the
'ties and offerings.'"

"I hear he was quite an Olympic athlete!"

"We were all out of bulletin paper."

"**O**kay, Bob...well—it looks as though your family troubles are all behind you."

"I just want to let you know, Harold, that except for the occasional, innocent slip to the mainstream media, everything you share in men's group is held in strict confidence."

"He comes in here for religious instruction every day—he's on the 'Frequent Friar' program."

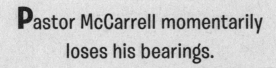

Pastor McCarrell momentarily loses his bearings.

"This button translates your words into Greek; this button mutes any coughs or burps; and this toggle emits an attention-grabbing, high-pitched frequency sure to raise the dead..."

"It's a pew glider."

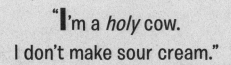

"**I**'m a *holy* cow.
I don't make sour cream."

"I have a chocolate problem."

Millie Fillmore inadvertently tithes a dish to pass.

129

Moses parts the red ink.

"**C**an I see your golden ruler?"

"In regards to tonight's fellowship potluck, remember the e-mail rule—no spam!"

"**S**o…do you get a weekly *pray*check?"

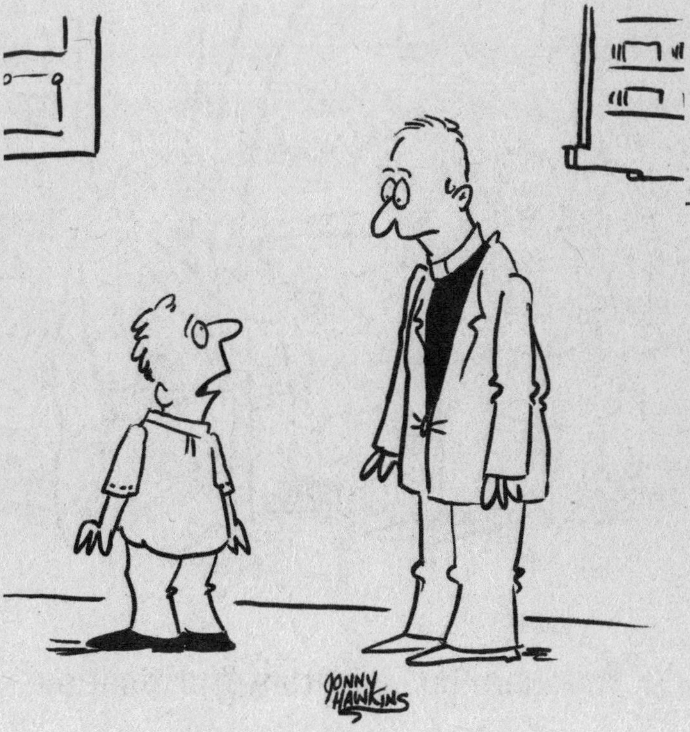

"**Y**our sermon on instant gratification didn't do anything for me."

The Church of Eternal Perspective
found a way to increase their
attendance *and* giving.

"**M**y husband and I wanted to let you know how much we appreciated the metallic funk-fusion influence in the worship music this morning, and that we were really moved by the subtle ska undertones blended with the moody mambo persuasion with just the right touch of hip-hop..."

"**H**ow did Jesus keep on loving people even when they drove him up a tree?"

"**E**veryone in the church looks so young.
Do you anoint them with Oil of Olay?"

"**M**y dad said that 'hallelujah' is Latin for 'the sermon is finally over.'"

"Since the church tank hasn't been cleaned, we're doing baptisms out here today."

"He's having his quiet time."

"Pastor, you'd be good at cards, since you really know when to fold your hands."

"In reference to the ancient passage in question, scroll down..."

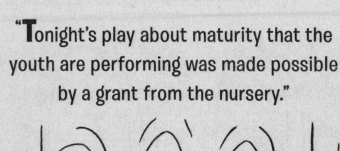

"Tonight's play about maturity that the youth are performing was made possible by a grant from the nursery."

"**D**o you earn a commission?"

"**P**astor, thanks for coming on such short notice."

"I fear commitment, but don't hold me to that."

"**A**nd here we go, ladies and gentlemen, with this week's top ten commandments..."

"The pastor's wife rearranged the furniture again."

"**B**less me, Father, for I have gone off my diet."